D0861492

KINGDOM RELATIONSHIPS

KINGDOM RELATIONSHIPS

God's Laws for the Community of Faith

Dr. Ron Moseley, Ph.D.

Lederer Books
a division of
Messianic Jewish Publishers
Clarksville, Maryland

Unless otherwise noted, all Scripture quotations are taken from the *Complete Jewish Bible*. Copyright by David H. Stern, Jewish New Testament Publications, Inc., 1998.

Also quoted is the NAS.

©2000 by Dr. Ron Moseley
All rights reserved. Published 2000.
Printed in the United States of America
Cover design by Now You See it! graphics

11 10 09 08 07   6 5 4 3 2

ISBN 10 1-880226-84-7
ISBN 13 978-1-880226-84-1
Library of Congress classification number 00-90048

No part of this publication may be reproduced, stored in a retrieval system, or transmitted in any form or by any means without the prior permission of the publisher, except for brief reviews in magazines, or as quotations in another work when full attribution is given.

Lederer Books
a division of
Messianic Jewish Publishers
P.O. Box 615
Clarksville, Maryland 21029

Distributed by
Messianic Jewish Resources International
Order line: (800) 410-7367
E-mail: lederer@MessianicJewish.net
Website: www.MessianicJewish.net

CONTENTS

PREFACE

The concept of the "Kingdom of God" is important to general readers, students, as well as professionals in every field who want information about early Christianity while it was still a sect of Judaism. This book has cut straight to the point and is divided into two sections. The first section consists of two chapters that introduce the relation of both the Jewish people and Christians to the Kingdom of God. The second section lists the laws that are applicable to a non-Jew living in the twenty-first century and outside of the land of Israel. Modern scholars have expended vast amounts of time and energy writing about the Kingdom of God. However, the primary inventory of the laws that Yeshua (Jesus) emphasized and their application as kingdom rules have remained elusive. To set the problem in perspective, this book provides a summary of the commandments for non-Jews and an analysis of some of the most important cultural differences affecting today's reader.

Why is this book needed? There are two basic reasons. First, these little-known laws of God's Kingdom were, according to Yeshua, the most salient features of the first-century community of believers. Yeshua even warned that anyone breaking these laws would be the least in the Kingdom (Matt. 5:19). Second, these laws will be the basis for the judgment at the end of every believer's life.

The biblical definition of sin is the transgression of one of these laws (1 John 3:4). Every first-century Jew understood Yeshua to be saying that the books being opened on Judgment Day were none other than the Book of Life and the record of our deeds according to the laws of God (Rev. 15:12; Eccles. 12:14). This very idea of opening books during a period of judgment was common in several ancient cultures, including the Egyptian and Babylonian cultures. These ancient cultures perceived these books as a record of human deeds and destinies, in light of the laws of their deities (*Mishnah Avot* ii.1, iii.20; Exod. 32:32; Ps. 69:29; Dan. 7:10; see Slotki, *Daniel, Ezra and Nehemiah*, p. 59; Rom. 14:10; 1 Cor. 3:11–15).

The purpose of this book is to provide a quick, easy-reading reference to these ancient laws. This is in the hope that they can be incorporated into the believer's life, producing life and peace in the highest form. To this end, there is a glossary of terms at the end of this book and questions at the end of each chapter that re-establish the major points.

INTRODUCTION

Since the time of Maimonides (the greatest of all Jewish philosophers; 1135–1204 c.e.), the general public has had clear access to the 613 laws of God as the rules for the Kingdom.

For years, my personal ministry, the Arkansas Institute of Holy Land Studies, has made a list of these rules available to interested believers. A problem arose almost immediately in distributing these ancient laws in a general form to a modern society. There needed to be a non-denominational, or non-theological, analysis explaining the different cultural trends that were taken for granted during the Temple periods.

This study attempts to make progress in two areas which will hopefully explain these rules of God's Kingdom in a manner beneficial to the scholar as well as the layperson. First, by examining the historical setting of the Kingdom and the concepts surrounding the Kingdom, this book lays a valuable foundation. It explains the origin of the Kingdom, including the role it played in ancient life, and the effect that its rules have on modern believers. Second, this book assumes that believers are more inclined to follow rules that are clearly defined. Thus, I have listed the laws which, in amiable consensus to Judaism and Christendom, make up the rules of God's Kingdom.

Section I

The Kingdom of God

CHAPTER 1

A Present Kingdom

The term "Kingdom of Heaven" (or "Kingdom of God") was a well-defined concept in the first century. Many contemporaries of Yeshua used this term. Some explained it as in the future; others, like Hillel (leader of a Pharisaic academy of higher learning) and Yeshua, understood God's Kingdom to be a present-day reality. Both the Zealots and Essenes viewed the Kingdom of Heaven as at hand, and saw themselves as active participants in the end-times drama that had already begun to unfold. Yeshua and the School of Hillel (the students of Hillel) believed that the Kingdom of Heaven could come about at any time in one's life, once the individual repented and took upon himself the yoke of the Kingdom.

In ancient times, the idea of taking on the yoke of something meant that one was linked in a partnership. In this case, the yoke of the Kingdom indicated a partnership with God the King. Jewish literature of Yeshua's day often mentions individuals taking on the yoke of the Torah and the yoke of the Kingdom.[1] At the moment that an individual takes on the yoke of the Kingdom, no nation or rule, except God's, can control that person. He or she becomes an active partner with God, fulfilling his promise to rule over Israel through his people, as they become servants to their King. Obedience to the laws of the land is simply a means of fulfilling the higher law of obedience to the Lord and his Kingdom.

Strife in the Kingdom

There were many factions of the Jewish faith during the first century. As in the Church today, not all were in complete unity with one another. None of these religious groups was more violent than the Zealots. Hatred and disunity arose in some groups who considered themselves a part of God's Kingdom. The Zealots' assault against fellow Jews, as well as against Rome, contributed to the destruction of the Second Temple.

The most violent of the Zealots was a group called Sicarri. They would walk among the Pharisees and other sects as if they belonged to them, and would suddenly draw a dagger and stab innocent bystanders. The Sicarri derived their name from the word *sica*, meaning a short, curved dagger. The leader of the Sicarri was Abba Sicara, the nephew of the great Pharisaic peacemaker Rabbi Yochanan Ben Zakkai. Sicara refused to follow his uncle's advice to make peace with Rome, and became a major factor in the war of 66–72 C.E.[2]

Taking the Kingdom by Force

A common and unfortunate English translation of Matthew 11:12 indicates that the Kingdom of Heaven suffers violence and the violent take it by force. Some, without knowing that the cultural and textual background of this statement came from Micah 2:13, have attributed violent, aggressive behavior to the Kingdom of God. Nothing could be further from the truth.

Amid the chaotic political and religious world of the first century, Yeshua and his followers understood that the Kingdom of Heaven had already begun with the work of John the Baptizer. John had broken forth into the Kingdom of Heaven as a "breaker" (leading lamb), breaking the sheep out of the sheepfold. This illustration was used by Yeshua in his *remez* teaching style (see Glossary), referring back to Micah 2:13. Yeshua was showing how the prophets of old functioned. Now the Kingdom of Heaven breaks forth and advances forcefully from within the dynamic movement of people who embrace the teachings of Yeshua and put them into practice (Matt. 11:12).

The Manifestation of the Kingdom

Yeshua declared that when he cast out demons, the Kingdom of Heaven had come (Matt. 12:28). The concepts of King and Kingdom were such an integral part of biblical Judaism that many prayers began with some variation of the words *Baruch atah Adonai Eloheynu melech ha'olam* ("Blessed are you, Lord our God, King of the universe"). This is still a formula used today in Jewish prayer. Even Yeshua's words incorporated the same formula, as he blessed the Father and prayed, "May your Kingdom come . . . on earth as in heaven" (Matt. 6:10). The rabbis believed in the divine kingship of God so strongly that they wrote, "any blessing that does not contain a mention of the divine kingship is no blessing."[3] This statement is found in the Jewish prayer book (*siddur*), which is over 2,500 years old, with some references to the Kingdom going back as far as 3,300 years.

The idea that the Kingdom of Heaven would manifest itself with miracles in the believer's life was not new. Before and during the first century, believing Jews, who depended on their King to show mercy in God's Kingdom, expected miracles. Many were familiar with the stories of Choni the Circle Maker, who drew a circle in the sand and refused to move until the Lord answered his prayer and sent rain.[4] Josephus, the Jewish historian, states that Choni had such a reputation for miracles that during the Jewish civil wars, one group sought his powerful prayers for military victory, and asked him to place a curse on Aristobulus (who was one of the warring pretenders for the throne). Being a man of faith in the King and Kingdom, Choni prayed: "O God, King of the universe, I beseech You not to hearken to them against these men nor to bring to pass what these men ask You to do to those others . . ." This caused the villains to stone him to death.[5] These stories were so much a part of first-century history that Yeshua alluded to the death of Choni in Matthew 23:37: "Yerushalayim! Yerushalayim! You kill the prophets! You stone those who are sent to you!"[6]

By Miracles the Kingdom Is Come unto You

The rabbis believed that God's Kingdom was established at the parting of the Red Sea.[7] Yeshua, in Matthew 12:28, declared: "But if I drive out demons by the Spirit of God, then the Kingdom of God has come upon you!" Others who believed in Kingdom miracles included the well-known Rabbi Chanina Ben Dosa. He successfully prayed that many be healed, and could tell whether his prayer for healing was going to be answered by a feeling he had during the prayer. Ben Dosa would say, "This one will live and this one will die."[8] Even famous Rabbi Yochanan Ben Zakkai asked Ben Dosa to pray for his sick son. When Ben Dosa put his head between his knees and prayed, the Lord healed the boy. Ben Zakkai's wife asked her husband why Ben Dosa had such power in prayer, and his answer was: "He is like a servant before the King," again revealing the Kingdom concept of the first century.

The popular Rabbi Gamaliel, teacher of the apostle Paul (Acts 22:3), sent his son to Chanina Ben Dosa for prayer. The boy was healed the same hour in which Ben Dosa prayed. This story is similar to the one of the centurion's son, who was healed the same hour in which Yeshua prayed for him (Matt. 8:13).

Miracles, as evidence of the power of the King in his Kingdom, were such a common sight among the Jews that sages recorded they were "accustomed to *nissim* [miracles]." This was said not only of famous teachers like Nahum of Gimzo, Simeon Ben Yochai, and Abba Chilkiah (the grandson of Choni the Circle Maker), but also of people such as the wife of Rabbi Chanina Ben Dosa and Beruria, the wife of Rabbi Meir.[9] Yeshua pointed to other rabbis doing miracles by his words to the Pharisees: "If I drive out demons by Ba'al-Zibbul, by whom do your people drive them out? So they will be your judges!" (Matt. 12:27)

There were at least four messianic miracles performed by Yeshua that ordinary rabbis could not duplicate. These included: 1) the cleansing of lepers, 2) the healing of a man born blind, 3) the casting out of certain demons that others could not drive out, and 4) the raising of a person who had been dead over three days. These miracles are covered in some detail in my book *Yeshua: A Guide to the Real Jesus and the Original Church* (see bibliography).

Rebellion: Throwing Off the Yoke of the Kingdom

Jewish scholar Johnnie Bradford points out that the rabbinic understanding of the Kingdom of Heaven is that it has always been present. Doing exactly what the children of Israel did at Sinai—submitting to do the will of God—brings about entrance into God's Kingdom. With one voice they said, "Everything that ADONAI has spoken we will do and obey" (Exod. 24:7). However, there were times when the children of Israel fell into rebellion. The rabbis understood this to mean the children of Israel rebelled against the Kingdom.[10] The incident of the Golden Calf, as well as the sins of Eli's two priestly sons, Hophni and Phinehas, are referred to by the rabbis as throwing off the yoke of God and denying the Kingdom of Heaven.[11]

The Kingdom of God is Near You

The significance of Yeshua's sending out of the seventy disciples and instructing them to heal, saying, "the Kingdom of God is near you" (Luke 10:8–9), is much clearer in the original Hebrew. If the reader does not recognize *karav* (come near) as the Hebrew equivalent of the Greek *engiken* (come near), he might think that the Kingdom is in the future. This is a classic example of a Hebrew term in Greek dress, which obscures the Hebrew meaning. Robert Lindsey, formerly of the Jerusalem School of Synoptic Research, addressed the meanings of the terms *karav* and *engiken* in Luke 10:9, when he wrote:

> This is when you need to know Hebrew! Sometimes Hebrew idiomatic usage explains difficult texts where the Greek translator of the Hebrew original simply rendered the Hebrew so literally into Greek that it makes sense in Hebrew, but not in Greek or English.[12]

An example where *karav* does not mean simply "to come near" can be seen in Isaiah 8:3, where it actually means "to be at."[13] In this text, Isaiah spoke of his sexual relations with his wife, saying: "So I approached [*karav*] the prophetess, and she conceived and gave birth to a son" (NAS). It is easy to see that the Hebrew understanding of the word *karav* means far more than our English translation "to come near."

A Progressive Kingdom Manifestation

As believers, we become subjects of the King, accepting the yoke of his Kingdom. We are conduits of God's healing love, through which his redeeming power touches a world in need. Dr. Brad Young points out that the Kingdom is the power of God at work to help people.[14] It is only through miracles and God's love in our lives that we can see the Kingdom of Heaven. Because each miracle is different, God's reign is constantly changing and progressive.

There are several major divisions among theologians concerning the Kingdom of Heaven. The two most popular are Dispensationalism and the "Kingdom Now" movement. Dispensationalism places the Kingdom in the millennium, at the conclusion of the present age. The "Kingdom Now" movement concludes that the Kingdom is established here on earth by human effort, paving the way for the Second Coming. However, in Yeshua's parables, he describes the Kingdom as the reign of God, a progressive force in the present world which he expects to be continued through his disciples.

Both the Parable of the Mustard Seed and the Parable of the Leaven depict the progressive growth of the Kingdom in our lives (Matt. 13). In essence, the Kingdom of Heaven can be described as God's reign among people who have chosen to follow his laws. As a result, God's redemptive purposes are manifested through them (Matt. 5:3; 6:33; Luke 11:20).

The Keys to the Kingdom

In Matthew 16:13–19, Yeshua asked Peter who is the Son of Man. Yeshua rewarded Peter's answer with the words: "How blessed you are! For no human being revealed this to you, no, it was my Father in heaven. . . . I will give you the keys of the Kingdom of Heaven." Yeshua rewarded Peter for acknowledging that Yeshua is the Messiah and affirmed that the work of the Kingdom is the work of Yeshua's disciples.

The power to "bind and loose" refers to first-century Jewish religious terminology that describes what the laws of the King (God) "forbid or permit." Jewish literature and the New Testament provide several examples of using the keys of heaven to bind and loose. The Sanhedrin reported that Choni the Circle Maker was known for binding and loosing. He used the words, "You have decreed on earth below and the Holy One, blessed be He, fulfills your word in Heaven above."[15]

First-century Jewish communities constantly called upon their rabbis to interpret scriptural commands and to decide moral dilemmas, much like a modern pastor. For example, the Bible forbids working on the Sabbath but does not define the specific activities that constitute work. Consequently, the rabbis ruled (bound or loosed) which activities they would permit, or not permit, on the Sabbath.

The Lord gave Peter the keys, or authority, to bind or loose concerning matters of scriptural interpretation, as seen in Acts 15. During the controversy over whether Gentiles could be admitted into the fellowship without being circumcised, Peter demonstrated loosing by ruling that both Jews and Gentiles were saved by faith (Acts 15:9). James, the leader of the Jerusalem congregation, demonstrated binding by requiring Gentile believers to abstain from the four characteristic practices of pagans (Acts 15:13–29).

Peter the Rock Is Based on Abraham the Rock

Yeshua taught many things based on well-known ancient Jewish stories. Regarding the Kingdom, Yeshua said, "You are Kefa [which means 'Rock'], and on this rock I will build my Community, and the gates of Sh'ol will not overcome it" (Matt. 16:18).

In Jewish literature, we discover a similar interpretation that helps us to understand this kingdom principle. In a story from *Yelamdenu*, a king dug deeply into several places seeking to find a foundation on which to build, but only found swamps and water. He refused to lay the foundation until he finally found a rock (in Greek, *petra*). He declared, "Here I will build. He laid the foundation and built!"[16] The story continues that God saw that Abraham would one day arise and use his faith, so he declared: "I have a rock upon which I can lay a foundation to build the world." Because Abraham believed and was credited with righteousness, God made him the foundation stone (little rock), and from Abraham God would make many rocks. The people of Israel believed Abraham was the Rock, after which the Children of Israel were to pattern themselves, and they became known as the rocks of the Rock. The relationship between Yeshua and his disciples should be understood in the same manner.

This is almost identical to Yeshua's statement following Peter's declaration of his Messiahship. Yeshua taught that he understood the Kingdom of Heaven to be made up of those who are doing the will of God (Luke 6:46). This concept parallels both the Jewish apocalyptic and rabbinic ideas that equate the Kingdom of God with the will of God. Likewise, when the people of God acknowledge his Kingdom principles, nothing can stop them, and the "gates of Sh'ol will not overcome it [their forceful entry]" (Matt. 16:18).

Abraham Renewed the Kingdom

Ancient rabbis taught that when sin came into the world, man's rebellion caused the flood. After the flood, the generations of Nimrod illustrated the Kingship of God by casting off the yoke of the Kingdom.[17] The Mishnah says, "The ungodly destroy the world while the righteous sustain it."[18] The rabbis taught that, with the call of Abraham, light returned to the earth, for he was the first to address God as "Master" or *Adonai*, declaring God's Kingship over the world.[19]

The ancient records say that Abraham brought the kingship of God to his generation. He thus established the precedent for it in the succeeding generations. As well, Jacob taught his children the yoke of the Kingdom of Heaven.[20]

The Miraculous: A Kingdom Principle

Yeshua often used the occasion of a miracle to illustrate the Kingdom of Heaven. Before working a miracle, he would make a pronouncement such as, "Courage, son! Your sins are forgiven" (Matt. 9:2). Yeshua did not teach that man was healed by faith, but as a result of the mercy of God, our supreme King, showing that the Kingdom had come in that situation. The reason that some of the Pharisees called this blasphemy was due to the fact that Yeshua used the word *salach*, a word showing that God had done the miracle, to indicate that the man's sins were forgiven. Modern scholars confirm that the word *salach* is used 42 times in the Hebrew Scriptures. Every usage indicates that God is doing the forgiving.[21] The key principle of Yeshua's miracle-working ministry is found in how he announced the Kingdom of Heaven: by declaring "Your sins are forgiven" and producing a miracle.

Brad Young points out that in Jewish texts, faith refers to the sovereignty of God. When snakes infested the people of Israel, God commanded Moses to erect a fiery serpent to bring a cure. According to the rabbis, it was not the fiery serpent who did the healing, but God. The people believed in the one who had commanded Moses to erect the fiery serpent.[22] Every miracle Yeshua performed was a declaration of the coming of the Kingdom of Heaven to his followers.

In Luke 11:20 ("But if I drive out demons by the finger of God, then the Kingdom of God has come upon you!"), the phrase "the finger of God" alludes to Exodus 8:15, which describes the miracles related to Israel's redemption from slavery in Egypt. In the days of Yeshua, a common Jewish belief held that a future messianic redemption would parallel Israel's redemption from the period of

Egyptian bondage. Just as the "finger of God" moved in Egypt, the "finger of God" moved when Yeshua performed messianic miracles. The experience of messianic miracles shows that the Kingdom of God has already "come upon you" (Luke 11:20).

Teaching Review, Chapter One

1.   Both the _____ and _____ viewed the Kingdom of Heaven to already be at hand and saw themselves as active participants in the eschatological drama that had already begun to unfold.

2.   In ancient times, the idea of taking on the yoke of something meant one was linked in a _____.

3.   Jewish literature often mentions individuals taking on the yoke of the _____ as well as the _____.

4.   The _____ were the most violent of the Jewish sects and eventually their careless hatred and disunity contributed to the destruction of the Temple.

5.   The most violent of the Zealots was a group called the _____.

6.   The leader of the Sicarri was Abba Sicara, the nephew of Rabbi Yochanan Ben _____.

7.   The word *Sicarri* came from the root word *sica*, meaning a short, curved _____.

8.   The unfortunate English translation of Matthew 11:12, which indicates that the Kingdom of Heaven suffers _____ and the _____ take it by force actually has a cultural background in Micah 2:13. This suggests that the Kingdom is like a leading lamb (breaker) breaking out of the sheepfold, and has nothing to do with violence.

9.   Yeshua often used the teaching style known as _____, meaning to hint or refer back to another text.

10. The Jews believe so strongly in the Kingdom principles that rabbis recorded that any blessing that does not contain a mention of divine kingship is no _____.

11. Choni the _____ is thought to be the one Yeshua is noting as being stoned in Matthew 23:37.

12. Rabbi Chanina Ben Dosa was famous for being able to pray and see God

heal the sick. Famous Rabbi Yochanan Ben Zakkai saw his sick _____ healed as Ben Dosa prayed.

13. In praying for the sick, Ben Dosa was given the ability from God to say: "This one will _____ and this one will _____."

14. In Jewish literature, _____ was understood to mean one was throwing off the _____ of the Kingdom.

15. It is easy to see that the Hebrew word *karav* means far more than what our English translation "to come near" portrays. This is illustrated when _____ the prophet used this word to approach his wife and she became _____.

16. Dispensationalists put the Kingdom in the _____ at the end of the present age.

17. Matthew _____, among other texts, establishes that the Kingdom of God is the progressive, present manifestation of God in our lives.

18. The power to "bind" and "loose" are Second Temple concepts meaning _____ and _____, referring to Jewish religious terms describing what the laws of God allow.

19. Referring to Peter as "a rock" possibly refers back to ancient Jewish history where _____ was known as the rock, after which the children of Israel were to pattern themselves.

20. The Pharisees called Yeshua's teaching blasphemous because he used the word *salach*, which was only used by _____.

21. In the days of Yeshua, it was a common belief that the messianic miracles would parallel the redemption of Israel from the _____ yoke. This appears to be behind Yeshua's use of the same phrase "The _____ of _____" as seen in Exodus 8:15.

CHAPTER 2

The Jewish Meaning of the Kingdom

When a Jew of the first century heard the term "Kingdom of Heaven," it triggered a *remez*, referring back to such texts as Exodus 15:18 and Psalm 93:1. These texts include the emphatic statement, "*Adonai* will reign forever and ever." This was so ingrained in their thinking that the rabbis referred to the phrase "*Adonai* will reign" as another term for "the Kingdom of Heaven."

To this Hebraic mindset, the "Kingdom of Heaven" is another way of conveying several theological ideas, including the following:

1. Obedience to God's laws
2. The reigning of the Lord over his subjects in love and healing
3. The deliverance of the King's people from every form of bondage
4. God's complete deliverance and protection of those in his Kingdom

Brad Young points out that the Kingdom of Heaven:

> . . . is not in heaven, it is not reserved only for the distant future. It does not begin in the millennium. The Kingdom of God is the power of God; that is, God doing what he wants, and the people of God doing what God wants. Yeshua said that the Kingdom was realized in the present when he worked a miracle. All people can experience God's rule when they obey God's absolutes. God's saving activity establishes his Kingdom now.[1]

Ancient Jews Avoided Using the Name of God

Although Jewish apocalyptic writings do not contain the actual term "Kingdom of Heaven," the concept is clearly defined. The terminology "Kingdom of Heaven" has its origin in rabbinic literature, where it refers to the Kingdom of God.[2] Jewish people during the time of Yeshua used the expression "Kingdom of Heaven" to avoid having to pronounce the name of God. "Kingdom of Heaven" became another way of saying "Kingdom of God." Yeshua used this phrase constantly, as recorded throughout Matthew.

The rabbis based this tradition on Exodus 15:18: "*Adonai* will reign forever and ever." The sages interpreted the phrases "I am *Adonai* [Yhvh; that is, God's ineffable name]" (Exod. 6:2–8; 14:4, 18), and "*Adonai* will reign forever and ever" to mean that Yhvh (that is, God himself) will rule over the Kingdom forever and ever.

The Kingdom Age

Many Christians have been taught, through sources such as the *Scofield Reference Bible*, that God has governed the world through seven different ages, or dispensations. We often refer to the last of these dispensations as lasting 1,000 years, and call it the "Millennium," or future age.

Robert Lindsey, the famous scholar from the Jerusalem School of Synoptic Research, points out that the teachings of Yeshua record only three ages. The first is called the "Age of the Law and Prophets" (Matt. 11). The second is referred to as the "Age of the Kingdom of God/Heaven" (Matt. 11; Luke 18). Finally, there is the "Age (World) to Come," (Hebrew *olam haba*), also called "Eternal Life" (Luke 18:30).

Yeshua spoke of the Kingdom of Heaven as his movement. What today is called the "Age of Grace" is actually the "Age of the Kingdom of God" (Matt. 11). Some dispensationalists have taught that, although Yeshua is both Lord and King, his Kingdom and earthly inauguration have been delayed until he can return with power to subdue his earthly enemies. Dispensationalists believe that at that time he will set up his Kingdom in Jerusalem with the restored Temple, where he will rule in the future. Actually, Yeshua taught that wherever he is worshipped as Lord, his Kingdom will reign, through healing, salvation, deliverance, and joy.

Later, Yeshua called his movement "the Church" (in Hebrew, his *Edah*, or witnessing body).

The King Parables

One of the most recurrent motifs of the Kingdom is the King (representing God), of which there are numerous permutations in "the King parables." Rabbinic literature has almost 5,000 parables, and more than 800 are King parables that are preserved from ancient times.

Yeshua used many King parables to illustrate the Kingdom of Heaven, many of which were similar to those used by his fellow Jewish teachers. For example, Rabbi Yochanan Ben Zakkai embellished the text of Ecclesiastes 9:8, which reads: "Let your clothing always be white, and never fail to perfume your head," with a King parable. The parable is of a king who announced an upcoming banquet without stating the time. Those who were discerning dressed for the occasion and waited, while the foolish went about their ordinary work, confident of being informed on time. Suddenly the summons came, and the wise entered dressed properly, while the foolish arrived in soiled garments. The king was pleased with the former and angry at the latter.[3] Rabbi Yochanan Ben Zakkai interpreted the parable to mean that a man should always be prepared to meet the Lord. This is remarkably similar to the King parable that Yeshua told concerning ten wise virgins and ten foolish virgins who went to the marriage banquet (Matt. 25).

More than a few of the rabbinic King parables have the same theme as the New Testament prodigal son parable, showing the King (God) as a loving father.

Accepting the Yoke of the Kingdoms

The Jewish people believed, as they recited the *Sh'ma* (Deut. 6:4: "Sh'ma, Yisra'el! *ADONAI* Eloheinu, *ADONAI* echad [Hear, Isra'el! *ADONAI* our God, *ADONAI* is one]") twice daily, that through this they were taking on the "yoke of the Kingdom of Heaven." They were "acknowledging that God is one and unique, and bearing witness that there is no other god."[4]

The Book of Jubilees (150 B.C.E.) records the episode of Abraham's conversion to Yhvh by declaring, "Thy Kingdom have I chosen."[5] The *Sh'ma*, one of the most sacred prayers, is believed to be a declaration of one's faith, much like the modern confession of faith in Christendom. Early sources suggest that the *Sh'ma* was the first portion of Scripture that Yeshua committed to memory. Records point out that Jewish boys were taught this biblical passage as soon as they could speak.[6] There are accounts of the *Sh'ma* being recited prior to the New Testament period; for example, the Letter of Artisteas (150 B.C.E.) refers to this fact. Mention is also made of the priests of the Temple period reciting it.[7]

During the first century, the School of Shammai (followers of Shammai, leader of a Pharisaic academy of higher learning in Jerusalem) held debates with the School of Hillel over the proper wording of the *Sh'ma*.[8] The *Sh'ma* was such an integral part of the life of the Jewish community that it was recited daily and was often used as a martyr's prayer at the time of death. When Yeshua was asked which commandment was most important, his reply was in line with this primary motif of Judaism; he quoted the *Sh'ma* (Mark 12:28–34; Matt. 22:34–40; Deut. 6:4–9).

Believers in ancient times maintained that bondage never came as a result of the active use of the law, but only from the unlawful use of, or breaking of God's laws. This idea is identical to those found in 1 Tim. 1:8 and 2 Tim. 2:5, which assure believers that it is beneficial to use the law properly. The Mishnah adds, in *Avot*,

> Whosoever accepts upon himself the yoke of the Torah takes on himself God's Presence and brings rest, and whosoever does not take upon himself the yoke of the Torah will have a time of hard labor.[9]

This sounds very similar to the words of Yeshua, as he reassured his disciples that his yoke is easy and brings rest, rather than being a heavy burden (Matt. 11:28–29). There is an interesting story in early Christian apocryphal literature stating that Yeshua had the quote "My yoke is easy" over his carpenter shop.[10] This illustrates the idea of Yeshua's emphasis on the yoke of the Kingdom so distinctly in his teachings.

Kingdom of Heaven and Kingdom of God

Jewish sages often used the term "Kingdom of Heaven" as a term for the sovereignty of God. Brad Young points out that the term "Heaven" means God himself. Yeshua taught, "But seek first his Kingdom and his righteousness."[11]

The name of God is probably the most often abbreviated word in Jewish writings. This is due to its frequent usage, where out of reverence alone it was condensed. Estimates indicate that there are over eighty substitutes for the Divine Name.

Examples of the word "Heaven" used as a substitute for the word "God" include:

1. "It is Heaven that rules"[12]
2. "In the sight of Heaven"[13]
3. "Let us cry to Heaven"[14]
4. "They are glorifying Heaven"[15]
5. "All the people adored and praised Heaven"[16]
6. "With the help of Heaven"[17]

The *Encyclopedia Judaica* points out that this usage is especially common in the Gospel of Matthew, where "Kingdom of Heaven" corresponds to "Kingdom of God."[18] This is also clearly seen in Luke 15:18, 21, where it says, "I have sinned against Heaven." The Pseudepigrapha abound with detailed descriptions of the Kingdom of Heaven, or the Kingdom of God, as it is also called.[19]

The term "Kingdom of Heaven" (Hebrew *Malkhut shamayim*; Aramaic *Malkhuta dishemaya*; Greek *Basileia ton ouranon*) has been a major concept within Jewish theology since the days of the pre-Maccabean sage Antigonus of Socho, 200 B.C.E.[20] In Jewish literature, "Heaven" substitutes for the name of God, as illustrated in: "fear of Heaven," "name of Heaven," and "for the sake of Heaven," or as a idiom for "God of Heaven" (Dan. 4:23).

The Kingdom Message: The Main Directive of the Torah

The rabbis commonly taught Israel to "take upon yourselves the yoke of the Kingdom of Heaven, treat one another in the fear of God and practice loving deeds" toward each other.[21] Jewish people from ancient times considered taking on the yoke of the Kingdom (by obeying the Torah) as just another way of expressing the same idea as "loving your neighbor as yourself." Yeshua taught the same in Matt. 19:19.

Joshua Ben Korcha declared that the first part of the *Sh'ma* (Deut. 6:4–9) preceded the second section (Deut. 11:13–22). Thus, believers could first take upon themselves the Kingdom of Heaven before taking on the yoke of the laws of God.[22] The Lord was primarily providing salvation, and secondarily providing, through his laws, a higher way of life for the subjects in his Kingdom.

The remainder of this book is devoted to God's laws that pertain to the present Kingdom of Heaven. Hopefully, categorizing and listing the laws of God's Kingdom, for easy access, will make life much less difficult for those who are really in pursuit of the King.

Teaching Review, Chapter Two

1. According to Dr. Brad Young, the Kingdom of Heaven is not in _____, nor is it reserved for the distant future, but it is present.

2. List two things that Dr. Young uses to describe the Kingdom of Heaven:
a. The _____ of God as seen by God doing what he wants.
b. The _____ of God doing what God _____.

3. The terminology "Kingdom of Heaven" has its origin in rabbinic literature where it refers to the _____ of _____.

4. In the day of Yeshua, the expression "Heaven" was used to avoid having to pronounce the _____ of _____.

5. Most Christians have been taught through sources such as the *Scofield Reference Bible* that God has governed the world through _____ different ages or dispensations. We often refer to the last of these as lasting _____ years and call it the _____.

6. Dr. Robert Lindsey points out that the teachings of Yeshua only recorded three ages: The first is called the age of the _____ and _____. The second is referred to as the _____ age. Finally there is the age to _____, called in Hebrew *ha'olam haba*.

7. What today is called the age of grace is actually the age of the _____ of _____.

8. The Hebrew word for the church was *Edah*, meaning a _____ body.

9. Rabbinic literature has almost _____ parables, and more than _____ of those are King parables.

10. Ancient Jews believed that when they prayed the _____ they were taking on the yoke of the "Kingdom of Heaven."

11. The *Sh'ma* was the ancient declaration of one's _____.

12. The Book of Jubilees (150 B.C.E.) records the episode of _____'s conversion to God.

13. Early sources suggest the *Sh'ma* must have been the first portion of Scripture _____ committed to memory.

14. During the first century, the School of Shammai held debates with the School of Hillel over the proper wording of the _____.

15. The *Sh'ma* was often used as a _____ prayer at the time of one's death.

16. When Yeshua was asked which commandment was the most important, he quoted the _____.

17. Ancient believers maintained that bondage only came from the _____ use or _____ of God's laws, and never because of the active use of the law.

18. The Mishnah records that whosoever accepts upon himself the yoke of Torah takes on himself God's _____.

19. Christian apocrypha records that _____ had this quote over his carpenter shop: "My yoke is easy!"

20. Dr. Brad Young points out that the term "Heaven" often refers to _____.

21. The name of _____ is probably the most often abbreviated word, due to its frequent usage in Jewish writings where, out of reverence, it was condensed.

22. It has been estimated that there are over _____ substitutes for the Divine Name.

23. Examples of the word "Heaven" used as a substitute for God include: "It is _____ that rules"; "in the _____ of Heaven"; "let us _____ to Heaven"; "all the people adored and _____ Heaven"; and "with the _____ of Heaven."

24. Ancient Jews considered taking on the yoke of the Kingdom by _____ the Torah.

Section II

Kingdom Rules for
Godly Relationships

CHAPTER 3

An Introduction to Understanding God's Laws
(Kingdom Rules)

Every kingdom has laws that govern the servants of the king. The Lord has provided 613 laws that govern his people in righteousness and peace. There are 365 commandments that teach "You should not" and 248 that teach "You should." All of these commandments govern believers. A large portion of these apply only to those living in the land of Israel, or living during either the First or Second Temple periods. However, there are 179 laws that I have personally applied to my life as a non-Jew living in the modern world, outside Israel. These relate to how I should treat fellow believers, and how to create a peaceful atmosphere, through obedience to my King.

Three Kinds of Commandments

The commandments of God are divided into three sections. The first consists of moral or ethical laws that are necessary for subjects of God's Kingdom to live together in harmony. These are known as *mishpatim*, which is generally translated "judgments." There are rituals and festivals that are intended to reawaken man to important religious truths. Among these rituals and festivals are the Sabbath, various feast days, guidelines concerning the *tefillin* (which are placed on one's forehead and left arm), and the *mezuzah* (which is attached to doorposts). These rituals and festivals fall into the second group, known as *eduyot*, which is translated "witnesses." The third group, called in Hebrew *chukim* ("decrees"), includes the moral, civil, and judicial laws.

As believers in Yeshua and servants in God's Kingdom, we are commanded to walk by faith and to fulfill the Law by applying its moral principles to our relationships with fellow believers (Matt. 5:17–20). Paul instructed Timothy that the Law was good if an individual used it lawfully, and that the only ones who would be crowned or rewarded would be those who lived lawfully (1 Tim. 1:8; 2 Tim. 2:5). Paul taught that he was not delivered from the Law of God, but rather was "within the framework of *Torah* as upheld by the Messiah" (1 Cor. 9:21). Standing before the high priest and Felix the governor, Paul boldly proclaimed that his accusers could not prove that he broke any of God's laws. Then, he confessed that he worshipped God and believed all things written in the *Torah* and the Prophets. Paul reminded his listeners that he continually brought offerings and alms and went through the Temple purification process (Acts 24:13–20).

Since we are not trained in the biblical mindset, there are many first-century Jewish terms relating to God's Law that Westerners find confusing. The Law was never intended to save anyone, but was designed for two purposes, which are both active today. The Law of God is so perfect that it immediately shuts the mouth of every sinner, and leads us to the Savior (Rom. 3:19; Gal. 3:21–24). The Law of God is also a standard for everyone in God's Kingdom to live by today, as well as a standard to be judged by at the end of time (Rev. 20:12–15).

The Nine-fold Purpose of the Laws of God

Realizing that we are in God's Kingdom and he is ruling believers through his relationship laws, it is imperative that his disciples understand the nine-fold universal aspects of God's Law.

1. The Law teaches believers how to serve, worship and please God (Ps. 19:7–9; Acts 18:13–14).
2. The Law instructs believers how to treat our fellow man, and how to develop healthy interpersonal relationships (Lev. 19:18; Gal. 5:14; 6:2).
3. The Law teaches believers how to be happy and prosperous by allowing God's power and authority to reign in our lives (Josh. 1:8; Ps. 1:1–3; Luke 12:32).
4. The Law is the measure of our deeds toward both God and our fellow man, guiding the way in all matters (1 Tim. 1:8–10; 2 Tim. 2:5; 1 Cor. 3:13; 6:1–12; Rom. 2:12; Rev. 20:12–13).
5. The Law is our schoolmaster, showing that we are guilty before God, and leading us to the Savior and King (Gal. 3:21–24; Rom. 3:19).
6. The Law reveals the existence of sin in the world, as well as the depth of our own sin (Rom. 3:20; 4:15; 7:7–8; Luke 20:47).
7. The Law reveals the good, holy, just, and perfect nature of God, as well as the universal standard of God's will for humanity (Rom. 2:17–18; 7:12; 2 Pet. 1:4).
8. The Law is to be established or accomplished through faith; hence, it is called the "Law of Faith" (Rom. 3:27–31, NAS).
9. The Law is written in our hearts by the indwelling Spirit of God. We can delight in and serve God through his Spirit (Rom. 7:6–25).

Great Christian Leaders Who Understood the Law

Martin Luther, the great reformer, declared,

> The first duty of the gospel preacher is to declare God's Law and show the nature of sin, because it will act as a schoolmaster and bring him to everlasting life which is in Jesus Christ.[1]

John Wesley said, "before I preach love, mercy, and grace, I must preach sin, Law and judgment." Wesley later advised a friend, "Preach 90% Law and 10% grace."[2] Charles Spurgeon, who is known as the Prince of Preachers, said, "They will never accept grace until they tremble before a just and holy Law."[3] Charles Finney, who is purported to have had an 80% success rate in his ministry, said,

Evermore the Law must prepare the way for the gospel; to overlook this in instructing souls is almost certain to result in false hope, the introduction of a false standard of Christian experience, and to fill the church with false converts.[4]

John Wycliffe, "the Morning Star of the Reformation," said, "The highest service to which a man may attain on earth is to preach the Law of God." D. L. Moody, who is credited with making more than a million disciples for the Lord, put it in perspective when he said, "God, being a perfect God, had to give a perfect Law, and the Law was given not to save men, but to measure them."[5]

Teaching Review, Chapter Three

1.   Every kingdom has laws that govern the king's servants, and the Lord has provided _____ laws that govern his people in righteousness and peace.

2.   There are _____ commandments from the Torah that could personally be applied to a non-Jew living in the modern world outside Israel.

3.   The commandments of God are divided into three sections. The first consists of _____ commandments, known as *mishpatim*, and are generally called judgments. The second group, known as *eduyot*, is translated as _____ because it lists such items as the *tefillin* and *mezuzah*. The third is called *chukim* or _____ and deals with civil and judicial laws.

4.   As believers in Yeshua and servants in God's Kingdom, we are commanded to walk by faith and to fulfill the _____ by applying its moral principles to our relationships.

5.   The Law was never intended to save anyone, but was designed for two purposes:
    a.   The Law of God is so perfect that it immediately shuts the mouth of every _____.
    b.   The Law leads us to the _____.

6.   List the nine-fold purpose of the Laws of God:
    a.   The Law teaches believers how to serve, _____ and please _____.
    b.   The Law instructs believers how to _____ their fellow man and how to develop healthy _____.
    c.   The Law teaches how to be _____ and _____.
    d.   The Law is to _____ our deeds toward both God and our fellow man.
    e.   The Law is our _____, showing us we are guilty before God and leading us to the _____.

f. The Law provides us with knowledge of what is _____.

g. The Law reveals the good, holy, just, and perfect _____
   of _____.

h. The Law is to be established and accomplished through
   _____.

i. The Law is written in our _____ by the indwelling Spirit of God,
   guiding us to delight in Him.

7. Name six great Christians who understood the Law:

   a. _____   b. _____
   c. _____   d. _____
   e. _____   f. _____

8. According to John Wesley, we are to "preach _____% law and ____% grace."

9. D. L. Moody said about the Law, "God being a perfect God, had to give a perfect Law, and the Law was given not to _____ men, but to _____ them."

CHAPTER 4

Personal Obligations to God

Laws Concerning Our Relationship with God

To become a believer in God in ancient times, one had to do three things to show his faith. First, the believer made a declaration of faith that Yhvh was the only God. This was done by saying the *Sh'ma*, the daily prayer: "Hear, Isra'el! ADONAI our God, ADONAI is one" (Deut. 6:4). Male believers also made this declaration by the act of circumcision. Second, a prescribed sacrifice was brought to the priest. Third, the believer was immersed in an immersion pool (Hebrew *mikveh*), equivalent to what Christians now refer to as "believer's baptism."

In the Second Temple period (New Testament times), Paul mentioned many baptisms, referring to the Jewish practice during the time of the early church (Heb. 6:2). Immersion was a part of numerous Jewish rituals, including purification of the believer before entering the Temple, purification of a woman after menstruation, sanctification of cooking utensils, and preparation for special events, to name just a few. Immersion was performed in order to have fellowship in the holy Temple precincts, to have contact with the priests, and to show bodily holiness to the one holy God. Beyond the ritual purity baptisms, there was only one baptism, called proselyte immersion, for new converts. It is this one "believer's baptism" that Paul mentions in Ephesians 4:5, and that Christianity continues to practice today.

Ancient Declaration of Faith

Outside of prayer and study, which will be discussed later, the ancient Jews had seven major items that constituted their declaration of faith. There are many recorded listings, but that of Philo (an Alexandrian Jewish philosopher of the first century), and a later compilation of the *Thirteen Principles of Jewish Faith* by Maimonides (the great Jewish thinker of the twelfth century), give us the basis for the following summary:

1. God is eternal and the only one to be worshiped (Exod. 20:2; Deut. 6:4).
2. Moses and the prophets were sent from God (Exod. 3:11–12; Judg. 6:8).
3. The Torah (Laws of God) will never be superseded or changed, taken away from or added to (Deut. 4:2; 12:32; Prov. 30:6; Matt. 5:17–19; Rev. 22:19).
4. God rewards those who fulfill the Torah commandments and punishes those who transgress them (Ps. 19:8–11; Matt. 15:3; 22:36–37; Mark 12:28–34; Luke 23:56; Eph. 6:2; James 2:9; 1 John 3:4).
5. The Messiah will come (Num. 24:17; Isa. 9:6; Mic. 5:2; John 1:36; 11:50–51).

6. Each person must repent of his or her sins (Job 42:6; 1 Kings 8:47; Ps. 51:1).
7. The dead will be resurrected (Job 19:25–27; Isa. 26:19; Ps. 16:10).[1]

Besides this declaration of faith, and the guidelines for the festivals and rituals, the ancient believers had only a few other direct commandments applicable to their relationship with God. These included:

1. To love God with all of one's heart (mind), soul (desires) and might (power or activities) (Deut. 6:5).
2. To fear, serve, and only swear by the name of the Lord (Deut. 6:13; 10:20). This was not a command to swear by his name, but actually a warning that if one is required to take an oath, he should do so only in the Lord's name, and not in the name of another god. It was believed that an individual could only swear by God's name while he feared, served, and cleaved to God (Deut. 10:20).
3. To sanctify or hallow his name openly by keeping the commandments (Lev. 22:32). In ancient times, three basic acts accomplished the idea of sanctification. First, sanctification was considered spiritual growth, by which a person increased in holiness. Second, sanctification was consecration (usually by a vow) of objects, persons or specific times, which were set apart for God. Third, sanctification was a formal acknowledgment of the name of God or days and festivals to honor him. The phrase "sanctification of the Name" became known as the acknowledgment of God's holiness through martyrdom. Jewish law teaches to preserve life at all costs, even if one must transgress the commandments of Torah. The exceptions to this are the laws concerning idolatry, murder, and adultery. Jewish sages believe that in the case of these three cardinal sins, one should endure martyrdom rather than transgress God's statutes.
4. To walk in the ways of God with all one's heart (Deut. 28:9). This is done by keeping the commandments.

Daily Prayer

Deuteronomy 6:13 and 11:13 remind us "to love *Adonai* your God and serve him with all your heart," which the Oral Law of the ancient sages interpreted to mean prayer, since "service with the heart" was done through prayer.[2] Daily prayer in the ancient Jewish world consisted of a number of things. First, the *Sh'ma* was recited every morning upon rising and every evening upon retiring (Deut. 6:7). The *Sh'ma* is made up of three texts: Deuteronomy 6:7; 11:13–21; and Numbers 15:37–41. It is considered the declaration of one's faith.

Prayer also consisted of blessing God (rather than the food), after each meal (Deut. 8:10). In addition, after the tithe was given, a declaration was made to the Lord with the words:

I have rid my house of the things set aside for God and given them to the Levite, the foreigner, the orphan and the widow, in keeping with every one of the *mitzvot* [commandments] you gave me. I haven't disobeyed any of your *mitzvot* or forgotten them. I haven't eaten any of this food when mourning, I haven't put any of it aside when unclean, nor have I given any of it for the dead. I have listened to what A*DONAI* my God has said, and I have done everything you ordered me to do. Look out from your holy dwelling-place, from heaven; and bless your people Isra'el [and whoever is praying] and the land you gave us [whatever we own], as you swore to our ancestors, a land flowing with milk and honey. (Deut. 26:13–15)

It is important to remember that the tithe was commanded. It was brought to the Temple in the land of Israel. I added it to my discussion on prayer because believers around the world should make a similar declaration upon bringing their money and gifts to the Lord.

Requirement to Study

Deuteronomy 6:7 commands each believer to "teach them [the laws of God] carefully to your children." Ancient Jewish society believed they were duty-bound to set a fixed time for Torah study both during the day and at night.[3] The Essene community at Qumran (c. 195 B.C.E. to 72 C.E.), where the Dead Sea Scrolls were found, had a company of hundreds of men divided into three shifts reading and studying the Scriptures around the clock. This activity was based on the exhortation in Psalm 1:2 to delight in the Law both day and night.[4]

The ancient Greeks studied for the sake of gaining knowledge, but the Hebrews studied to maintain reverence for God. During the first century, study was considered one of the strongest forms of worship. Paul echoes this with the phrase: "Be diligent to present yourself approved to God" (2 Tim. 2:15). The most sacred religious object in ancient Israel was the Holy Ark, which housed the two tablets of the Torah. Even today, when the ark is opened to study the scrolls in a synagogue, the people stand to their feet as they did in Nehemiah's day (Neh. 8:5).

In the Hebrew language, the word *avodah* means both work and worship. In Judaism, both study and prayer are considered worship, as is the work at the altar. The Jewish sages in their writings refer to "education" as a synonym for "heavenly work."

In ancient Judaism, there was a famous debate whether studying or doing good deeds was more important. The conclusion was that study superseded charity because it leads to observance.[5] The basic laws concerning study are summarized in three areas:

1. To learn Torah and teach it to your children (Deut. 4:9; 6:7).
2. To write a Torah scroll for yourself (Deut. 31:19). If one could not write the scroll made up of the Torah commandments, then he was allowed to purchase one. The basic idea was that each individual was responsible for having and putting to memory the concepts of the Torah laws. The Jewish sages

believed that if a person altered one letter of the Torah scroll, it was as though he changed the whole Torah.

3. To be attached to Torah scholars and their disciples (Deut. 10:20). The ancient sages taught that the phrase "and to Him [God] shall you cling" was accomplished by sitting under a Torah scholar. The sages also believed that each person should spend time with his Torah scholar, including such events as eating with him and permitting him to benefit from the student's wealth. It was said, "he should wallow in the dust of the feet of Torah scholars, and drink in their words thirstily."[6] The ancient sages, as well as Yeshua, command that we go forth and make disciples through studying and teaching (Matt. 28:19–20; *Avot* 1:12).

Laws Against Paganism and Idolatry

It is forbidden for believers to make any image of a human, animal or fowl for the purpose of worship (Exod. 20:20; Lev. 20:23). It is also forbidden for a believer to have in his possession anything worshiped by pagans. Other commandments regarding this subject in the Torah state that:

1. A believer is not to set up a pillar or other item used in pagan worship (Deut. 16:22).
2. A believer is not to tattoo or mark his body in any way, as was commonly done in worship by the pagans (Lev. 19:28). The penalty for this was lashes from a whip, but the individual could repent and receive forgiveness, as with any of these offenses.
3. A believer is not to shave his head for religious purposes, as was the custom of the heathen (Deut. 14:1).
4. A believer is not to practice augury, or foretell the future by interpreting omens (Lev. 19:26). This includes other things such as conjuring or soothsaying, divination, sorcery, casting charms and spells, and consulting a medium, wizard, or a necromancer (Deut. 18:10–11; Lev. 19:31).
5. A believer is forbidden to prophesy falsely in the name of the Lord (Deut. 18:20).

Joy in Worship

Believers are commanded to rejoice when coming before the Lord with offerings, for worship or during festivals (Deut. 16:14; 26:14). When ancient Jewish believers entered the Temple, they were forbidden to come without an offering or without joy (Deut. 16:16).

Some of the offerings were called "peace offerings of rejoicing."[7] The water-drawing ceremonies were filled with dancing and laughter, so much so that it was said by those in attendance that whoever did not participate in this had never experienced real rejoicing in his lifetime (John 7:8).[8]

One of the reasons for curses falling on the ancient believers was their neglect to serve the Lord with joyfulness, resulting in their lack of abundance of all things (see Deut. 28:47).[9] Yeshua taught this same concept concerning believers having life and having it more abundantly (John 10:10; Luke 2:10; 8:13; Matt. 25:21–23).

Fear and Reverence for God and Man

Ancient Jewish society, including Yeshua, believed that a holy fear and respect followed all that was affiliated with God. The believers studied the Torah laws with the expectation that it would produce reverence. It is not difficult to see where the reverence has gone, since most of Christendom has replaced God's laws with modern theology. Yeshua told us that in God's sight the teaching of God's laws determines greatness, and the lack of it causes us to be diminished (Matt. 5:17–20). The basic laws concerning reverence are summarized in the following three groups:

1. Believers are to have a fear of God and his sanctuary (Lev. 19:30; John 5:23; 8:49). Even today the synagogues and Houses of Study are called "little sanctuaries" (Ezek. 11:16). Since God dwells inside believers, this same courtesy should be extended to all believers (Exod. 25:8; 2 Cor. 6:16).
2. Believers are to keep a special day (Sabbath) to honor the Lord (Lev. 19:30; Luke 4:16). There is disagreement whether Christians should keep the Sabbath or worship on Sunday. Since the purpose of this book is not to establish doctrine, this is not the place to address such a theological debate. As a concise statement of biblical fact, it should be noted that observing the Sabbath was never a part of salvation, but a means to honor the Lord and rest from regular work in his name (Exod. 23:12). There is no indication that believers are to hold a synagogue or church service on the Sabbath.
3. Believers are to rise for an aged person, as well as stand to honor a Torah scholar, when he enters our presence (Lev. 19:32). We are commanded to honor many in authority, including our wives and husbands, prophets, our fathers and mothers, government officials, members of our spiritual community, and widows.

Ministers who teach well are worthy of double honor (Mark 6:4; 7:10; 1 Cor. 12:23; 1 Tim. 5:3,17; 1 Pet. 3:7). In ancient times, everyone was commanded to honor the priesthood. Indeed, Moses had sanctified them by setting them aside for the work of God (Lev. 21:8). Later records indicate the priests were honored in several ways, including being first to be seated at meals and first to say the benediction at a meal, even if doing so was against his will. This is not to say that we should do the same thing today with ministers, but we can easily see this principle in honoring the men and women of God.

Teaching Review, Chapter Four

1. To be a believer in God during ancient times, one had to do three things:

    a.   Make a _____ of faith that Yhvh was the _____ God (and males had to be circumcised).

    b.   Make a _____.

    c.   Be _____ in a *mikveh*.

2.   In the Second Temple period, Paul mentioned many baptisms, referring to the Jewish practice concerning ritual purity. Besides the various forms of ritual purity, there was only one baptism called _____ immersion for new _____.

3.   Outside of prayer and study, the ancient Hebrews had seven major items that constituted their declaration of faith:

    a.   God is the only one to be _____.

    b.   Moses and the _____ were sent from God.

    c.   The Torah Laws will never be _____.

    d.   God _____ those obedient to the Torah.

    e.   _____ will come.

    f.   Each person must _____ of his or her _____.

    g.   The _____ will be _____.

4.   We sanctify or hallow God's name openly by _____ the _____.

5.   In ancient times, the idea of sanctification was accomplished in three basic acts:

    a.   Spiritual _____ by increasing in _____.

    b.   By the consecration of a _____.

    c.   By a formal acknowledgment of the _____ of _____.

6.   The phrase "sanctification of the name" became known as the acknowledgment of God's holiness through _____.

7.   Ancient Jewish law teaches that it was permitted to break any of the Torah laws in order to preserve a life—with the exception of these three:

    a.   _____   b. _____

    c.   _____

8.   The phrase "to walk in the ways of God with all of one's heart" meant to _____ the _____.

9.   The phrase "service with one's heart" meant to _____.

10. The believer is to bless _____ rather than the food and to do it _____ each meal.

11. After each tithe was given, a _____ was made to the Lord.

12. The Torah commands each believer to _____ the Laws of God to your _____ (Deut. 6).

13. The Essene community (where the Dead Sea Scrolls were found) had a company of hundreds of men divided into three shifts _____ the _____ around the clock, based on Psalm 1:2.

14. The ancient Greeks studied to _____, while the Hebrews studied to maintain _____ to God.

15. During the first century, _____ was considered one of the highest forms of worship.

16. The most sacred religious object in ancient Israel was the holy _____ that housed the _____.

17. People stood as the Word of God was read as far back as _____ day (400 B.C.E.).

18. In Hebrew, the same word (*avodah*) means both _____ and _____.

19. The Jewish sages in their writings refer to _____ as heavenly work.

20. In ancient Judaism, there was a famous debate whether studying or doing good deeds was more important. The conclusion was that _____ superseded because it led to _____.

21. The basic laws concerning study are summarized in three areas:

    a.   To learn _____ and teach your _____.
    b.   To write a _____.
    c.   To attach oneself to a _____.

22. It was forbidden for any believer to make an image of a human, animal or fowl for the purpose of _____ or to have in one's possession anything _____ by pagans (Exod. 20; Lev. 20).

23. It was forbidden for a believer to _____ or mark his _____ in any way common to pagans (Lev. 19). The penalty for this was lashes with the whip, and after repentance, it was forgiven.

24. A believer was not to _____ his _____ for religious purposes as was the custom of the heathen (Deut. 14).

25. A believer was not to _____ the _____ by means of any type omens (Lev. 19). Along this line, a believer was forbidden to _____ falsely in the name of the Lord (Deut. 18).

26. Believers were commanded to _____ when bringing offerings, in worship and during festivals (Deut. 16; 26). Two things a worshiper could not approach the Temple without were _____ and _____ (Deut. 16). Some of these offerings were actually called "Peace offerings of _____."

27. One of the reasons for curses falling on ancient believers was their neglect to serve the Lord with _____, resulting in their lack of _____ in all things (Deut. 28).

28. Yeshua taught that in God's sight the teaching of _____ _____ determines greatness and the lack of it causes us to be diminished (Matt. 5).

29. The synagogues are referred to as _____ (Ezek. 11:16).

30. Although the Sabbath was never a part of _____, it was established to honor the Lord. There is no biblical indication that believers are to hold a _____ on the Sabbath.

31. Believers are commanded to rise before an _____, as well as stand to honor a Torah scholar, when they enter our presence (Lev. 19).

32. Ministers who _____ well are worthy of double honor (1 Tim. 5).

33. Because of the biblical honor of the priesthood, later Jews come to honor them in special ways, such as preferring them first at _____, among other things (Lev. 21).

CHAPTER 5

Proper Relationships Among Believers

Love and Covenant Relationship between Believers

In ancient times, the believer was required to give to the poor. This comes from several texts, but especially Deuteronomy 15:8, where believers are commanded to give to the needy. Literally, this text says, "opening, you shall open your hand," which denotes that one must help the needy repeatedly. If a brother refuses charity, we are to advance him a comparable amount of money as a loan, based on the final words of the text, which state, "and [you shall] lend him enough to meet his need."

Jewish people were to handle giving with at least the same diligence as in private money matters. If an individual did not have the means to support every charitable cause, the first priority was to give to poor relatives. If possible, one should then help the poor among his neighbors, the poor of his own city, and finally the poor of his own country. The poor of Israel took precedence over the poor of another people outside of Israel. This form of giving is called *tzedakah* in Hebrew, taken from the root of the word for doing a righteous deed. This was to be done in a friendly manner and with encouraging words. Paul alludes to this in 2 Corinthians 9:7 by using the words "cheerful giver."

The poor man sustained by such charity had a duty to give charity in some fashion to someone else. Those among the poor man's relatives took precedence over the poor of his town. The poor of his town took precedence over the poor of another town. This was based on the text: "You must open your hand to your poor and needy brother in your land" (Deut. 15:11). Ancient Jewish literature treated the person who hid his eye from the penniless person seeking help as a scoundrel, a sinner, and a wicked person. The Apostle Paul exhorted that the greatest of the gifts are faith, hope, and charity, and that charity takes precedence (1 Cor. 13:13). The implication of this statement is that charity involves giving to others, and is not selfish.

We are to love our neighbors as ourselves, as Yeshua reminded us when he quoted Leviticus 19:18 (in Matt. 7:12). In examining the Leviticus text, we see what Yeshua and others of his day already knew: that the surrounding text defines how to accomplish this love. In short, we are to love our neighbor by:

1. not holding a grudge against a brother and not hating him;
2. refusing to talk about him or sow discord by discovering his evil and/or communicating it to others;
3. rebuking him through encouragement while not embarrassing him;
4. not taking revenge for anything done to ourselves or someone else (Lev. 19:16–19).

As believers, we are not to oppress fellow believers with our words or actions (Lev. 25:17). This command in its original meaning covers such areas as purposely offending someone or hurting someone's feelings, causing stress, or even deceiving someone.

There is special attention given to commands not to offend, hurt, neglect, criticize, or mock widows, orphans, the blind, and the deaf (Exod. 22:22; Lev. 19:14). Since widows, orphans, the blind, and the deaf are vulnerable, either because of their obvious handicap or because they have no husband or father to protect them, the Lord commands his people to do more on their behalf. Since the word "blind" is a Hebrew idiom and metaphor for both those who cannot physically see and for any unsuspecting person, "blind" in this text commands believers not to cause anyone to stumble over anything (Lev. 19:14).

One should note the five different kinds of widows mentioned in 1 Timothy 5:

1. Any widow who "has children or grandchildren" (verses 3–4, 8) or "has relatives" (verse 16), and thereby should be cared for by her family;
2. "The widow who is really in need" (verse 5), who could qualify to be helped by the community of faith;
3. A widow who gives herself "to wanton pleasure" (verse 6, NAS), who is immoral;
4. A widow "more than sixty years old" (verses 9–10);
5. "Younger widows" (verses 11–15), who should remarry.

It is forbidden for any believer to tell a second person derogatory things which were said of him by a third person (Lev. 19:16). If this principle alone were followed, it would revolutionize the world of believers.

As believers, we are commanded not to refrain from rescuing our fellow man from danger (Lev. 19:16). Ancient Jewish society believed that this applied not only to such dangers as drowning, or monetary loss, but also to dangers such as robbery or a life that is being threatened. We have a responsibility to pacify the thief or murderer, or do whatever is within our ability to save the innocent individual.

We are not to leave the animal of a fellow believer lying crouched under its load, and hide ourselves from the responsibility of helping unload the animal (Deut. 22:4). Since the ancient animal was used in making a living, this could and should apply today to a vehicle or instrument of one's business or travel.

If a believer sees an animal or object that another believer has lost, he is forbidden to ignore it, and is required to return it to the owner. If the owner lives far away, the believer is to inform the owner, and care for the animal or object as though it were his own until the owner comes to retrieve it (Deut. 22:1–3).

There are even laws to guard the land during a war. It is forbidden to destroy any fruit-bearing tree during a siege (Deut. 20:19). God gave this law for many reasons, not the least of which was because these trees were to help provide for the poor and unfortunate of the community.

A believer is to make safety provisions around his dwelling to remove every potential cause of an accident (Deut. 22:8).

It is forbidden for a believer to lie or swear in vain to do something which cannot be accomplished, or to swear falsely over a business deal (Exod. 20:7, 16; Lev. 19:11).

It is forbidden to lust after or covet that which belongs to another (Exod. 20:17). There are nine major types of lust mentioned in the biblical text:

1. lust to destroy (Exod. 15:9);
2. lust for strong drink (Deut. 14:26);
3. lust for what is not provided (Ps. 106:15);
4. sexual lust (Matt. 5:28);
5. lust for the spirit of the world (Mark 4:19);
6. lust of the devil (John 8:44);
7. homosexual lust (Rom. 1:27);
8. lust for things that do not belong to oneself (Rom. 7:70);
9. lust to have one's own way (Titus 3:3; Jude 1:18).

It is forbidden for believers to commit premeditated murder, or to kidnap any living person (Exod. 20:13).

It is forbidden for believers to strike or curse one another (Deut. 25:3; Exod. 21:15, 17; Lev. 19:14).

It is forbidden for a believer to wrongfully retain anything belonging to his fellow man (Lev. 19:13).

It is forbidden to cheat in any business deal, or move real estate boundaries (Lev. 19:35; Deut. 25:13–14; 19:14).

It is forbidden to hate a brother in your heart, to do anything purposely to cause him to stumble spiritually or physically, to bring shame to his life, or to take revenge for something he has done to hurt you (Lev. 19:14, 16–18).

It is forbidden for a believer to curse or appoint a corrupt judge, or to be involved in rendering an incorrect judgment in a court case (Deut. 1:17; Exod. 23:1, 3, 6). It is equally forbidden for a believer to be a corrupt judge, rendering any perverted justice according to his personal opinions or prejudices (Deut. 19:15; 24:16–17; Exod. 23:1, 3, 6, 8; Lev. 19:15).

Loans and Money Matters between Believers

We are to loan or give to the poor believer when he is in need, when we have the means to help (Deut. 15:7). This applies especially to our relatives and those within our city or community of faith. We are forbidden to turn a blind eye once we are aware of a fellow believer's distressing financial situation. Although sometimes we are unable to solve his problem completely, we are in some way to demonstrate compassion and goodwill. Likewise, the individual being helped is required to actively help others.

Ancient Jewish believers were not allowed to charge interest on a loan to a fellow believer as they would a non-believer (Exod. 22:25; Deut. 23:19–20). This principle is referred to in Luke 6:34–35, where the indication is that believers are not to do as unbelievers and profit from interest charged to believers. One major concern in this area is that a loan with non-payable interest makes the borrower a servant to the lender, instead of brother (Prov. 22:7).

A believer is not to demand a borrower to pay his debt immediately when the lender knows he does not have the means to pay the debt (Exod. 22:25). The English translation is not as clear on this text, but the Hebrew conveys the idea of a believer not being a collector as well as not charging interest. This does not mean the lender is to suffer because the borrower is unscrupulous and is failing to pay due to mismanagement or dishonesty. Just as the lender is forbidden to make demands, so is the borrower forbidden to suppress the money which is due to his fellow man.

The Jewish believers had a *Bet Din*, or religious court, in which a believer acting like an unbeliever was made to pay the debt. Paul alludes to this in 1 Corinthians 6:1, when he rebukes believers for going to a worldly court instead of bringing personal matters before the *Bet Din*. Such matters were not brought openly before the local congregation, but each synagogue or group of believers had a minimum of a three-man court based on God's laws to deal with questionable matters (see below).

Relationships between Employers and Employees

The employer was to allow the employee to eat of the produce in which he was working, when it was something that grows from the ground. The employer was to give wages to an employee on the same day as earned, if he was in need and asked for it (Deut. 23:25; 24:15). Although the employee was permitted to eat of the produce in which he worked, he was not to do it during work hours. The employee was not to take more from the field than what he personally could eat at one meal. He was not to take away food in his hand or in a container, nor was he to give it to others (Deut. 23:26).

Fulfilling Vows and Pledges

God commanded us always to fulfill every word that comes from our lips. This applies whether those words are in the form of a vow, a pledge, or just a spoken commitment. Ancient Jewish society, in accordance with the biblical precepts and spirit to do all things honestly before mankind, did permit an individual to come before a Jewish court. The court would then determine if, under specific conditions and only if the Law permitted, a vow or pledge could be withdrawn or nullified. The nullifying of a vow had to be done before a *Bet Din*. The court had to be well acquainted with God's laws and able to render a decision accordingly.

This ruling was based on the writings found in Numbers 30, and the individual had to confess his regret over making the vow, as well as his reason for wanting to nullify the vow. He then had to ask to be forgiven before any decision concerning the vow could be made.

As part of ancient pledges, a pawn of some important object was made to guarantee payment. A believer was not allowed to take any of the following items as a pawn: utensils used to support a family, any object by force, a garment or other needed items from a widow or person in need. Even the lender was not to take back an item by force from a borrower, except by a ruling of the religious court. It is also forbidden to withhold an object which was taken in pledge from its owner if the owner truly needs it (Deut. 24:10, 12, 17).

In addition, it was forbidden for any believer to delay in presenting a vowed or voluntary offering (Deut. 23:21–22).

The Court in the Local Congregation

Records tell us that the Roman government permitted Jewish communities to settle their own disputes in money matters and things pertaining to this life (see 1 Cor. 6:4).[1] One such example is given by the Roman proconsul Gallio, the elder brother of Seneca, who was Nero's tutor (Acts 18:15). Gallio permitted Jewish subjects to render their own judgment according to God's law.

The early church was based on Jewish principles and patterned after the Jewish synagogue, including the use of a seven-man judicial panel (Acts 6:3). It is probable that Paul is referring to this type of religious court passing judgment using God's laws in congregations like that at Corinth, where Jews as well as God-fearers had embraced the Good News of the Messiah. It is not realistic to think that Paul, trained as a Pharisee of the Law, would set up a congregation with any other type of court system (1 Cor. 6:1). Further evidence of this Jewish court system is seen in the terms used in 1 Corinthians 6:4: "no standing" and "matters of everyday life." These are similar phrases used by Jewish courts in reference to a lower panel of three judges found in every synagogue.

John Lightfoot (a 17th century scholar) and Adam Clark (an 18th-19th century theologian and scholar) seem to agree that Paul is referring to this lower Jewish court which was also implemented in the Corinthian church.[2] In Deuteronomy 24:9, these judges were called "elders." Jewish society, of which Paul was a part, considered a believer who took his case before the gentile courts to be profaning the name of God. Their general rule was: "He who tries a cause before the judges of the Gentiles, and before their tribunals, although their judgments are as the judgments of the Israelites, so this is an ungodly man."[3] With this same idea, Paul is saying to the Corinthian church: "How dare one of you . . . go to court before pagan judges . . . (1 Cor. 6:1)

Care of Animals

God's laws are so detailed that they include provisions for animals.The following teach some of these provisions:

1.   Believers are forbidden from even taking the eggs from a bird's nest while the mother bird is present (Deut. 22:7).
2.   A believer is forbidden to take the mother bird and her young from the same nest (Deut. 22:6).
3.   A believer is forbidden to muzzle an ox while it is working in the grain (Deut. 25:4). Paul mentions this well-known principle to both Timothy and the Corinthians (1 Cor. 9:9; 1 Tim. 5:18).
4.   Believers are not to leave an ox or needy animal in a ditch or in jeopardy (Luke 14:5; Exod. 23:5).
5.   A believer is forbidden to leave an animal, even that of an unbeliever, laboring under an unjust burden without helping it (Exod. 23:5).

There are 42 different animals mentioned in Scripture. God not only had Adam name each animal, but declared that his covenant includes them (Gen. 2:20; 9:9–10). Even the sparrow which falls to the ground is noted by God (Matt. 10:29; Luke 12:6).

Not only is man to rest on the Sabbath, but the same provisions are made for the animals (Exod. 20:10). The righteous individual regards the lives of his animals and cares for them, while the person who fails to do so is considered wicked by the Lord (Prov. 12:10).

Marriage and Biblical Sexual Relationships

Believers were commanded to marry and to sanctify the home with true love (Gen. 1:28; 2:23–24; Deut. 24:1).

In ancient marriage contracts, the husband was obligated to provide his wife with three major things, which are listed in Exodus 21:10. In short, these included sexual relations, food, and clothes. On a much broader level, these have come to include various laws of the sages involving all of the biblical principles. These laws of the sages are summarized in the following seven marital obligations:

1.   The husband must make the principal payment of the marriage contract.
2.   He must provide medical care.
3.   He must pay a ransom for his wife if she is taken captive.
4.   He must bury his wife when she dies.
5.   If he should die first, she is to stay in his house for the remainder of her life.
6.   She is to be sustained out of his property.
7.   Her children are to be sustained out of his property until they become betrothed.[4]

A number of sexual abuses are listed in detail in order to protect the marriage and safeguard the believer from falling back into the many pagan sexual practices associated with idolatry. Those related to the general public include what is called "a forbidden consanguineous relation." This is when a believer approaches any one of his relatives to uncover their nakedness or do anything sexual that may lead to an improper fantasy or conjugal intimacy (Lev. 18:6). This would include any form of incest as we know it today.

The following Torah commands also relate to improper sexual relations:

1. A believer is not to uncover the nakedness of his father in homosexual intimacy (Lev. 18:7).
2. A believer is not to be intimate with his mother (Lev. 18:7).
3. A believer is not to be intimate with his father's wife (Lev. 18:8).
4. A believer is not to be carnally intimate with his father's brother (Lev. 18:14).
5. A believer is not to be intimate with his daughter-in-law (Lev. 18:15).
6. A male believer is not to have carnal intimacy with another male (Lev. 18:22). If this was done, a sin-offering was required. Modern laymen often take Paul's comment that the effeminate will have no part in the life to come as a judgment that this sin cannot be forgiven. How sad! Paul is simply saying this is a sin, and no sin will be permitted in the Kingdom of Heaven. Any sin can be forgiven through confession and repentance (1 Cor. 6:9).
7. A believer (male or female) is to have no carnal intimacy of any kind with an animal (Lev. 18:23).
8. A believer is not to be intimate with any of his or her grandchildren (Lev. 18:10).
9. A believer is not to be intimate with a woman and her daughter, or a woman and her granddaughter (Lev. 18:17).
10. A believer is not to be intimate with a woman who is married to someone else (Lev. 18:20).
11. A believer is not to be intimate with his aunt or uncle (Lev. 18:12, 14).
12. A believer is not to be intimate with the wife of his brother or half brother, or sister or half sister (Lev. 18:9, 16).
13. A believer is not to be intimate with his sister or brother (Lev. 18:11).
14. A believer is not to be intimate with the sister of his wife (Lev. 18:18).
15. A believer is not to be intimate with a harlot without a marriage (Deut. 23:18).
16. If a man seduces a virgin who is not engaged to him and has sexual relations with her, he has to pay a dowry of fifty shekels of silver to her father. If her father permits it, the man has to marry her (Exod. 22:16–17). Fifty shekels were equal to approximately one hundred days of work at common labor.

Although polygamy was permitted in antiquity, and still is in several countries, it was never God's intention. Kings and spiritual leaders were not to have more than one wife at one time (Deut. 17:15, 17; 1 Tim. 3:1–2).

Pagan worship in ancient times included pornography in the form of statues, sexual symbols, and cult prostitutes, which allowed the people to pay tithes in heathen temples through sex. Thus, there are various decrees from the Lord to destroy all such places. These pillars, groves of trees (Hebrew *asherim*), and obelisks were phallic representations, and were offensive to believers and to God.

There are several other precepts that have to do with Jewish law in ancient times that are not listed with these, but could apply to the non-Jew in modern times under special circumstances. These include such laws as not taking back one's divorced wife once she has been married to another man (Deut. 24:4), not to be conjugally intimate with a woman who is ritually unclean due to menstruation (Lev. 18:19), and not to castrate any male creature because to do so rendered it unfit for service in the Temple as a sacrifice or servant (Lev. 22:24).[5]

The Biblical Divorce

If a divorce was desired for some biblical reason (that is, some uncleanness found in the marriage, such as one party breaking some of the laws of God), the offended party could bring the other to the religious court, and the judges would render a divorce.

The often-quoted text of Malachi 2:16, which appears to read "God hates divorce," is actually misused. This text actually states that God hates the pagan custom of divorce. This custom was not a biblical divorce, but involved simply "putting away" or "turning out" a wife without appearing before a religious court and without rendering just and godly compensation. This passage of Scripture was referring to believers who were following the pagan practice of "putting away" their Jewish wives to marry pagan women. The pagans did not require compensation or an official divorce decree from a religious court of judges using God's protective laws. This destructive practice violated God's divorce law found in Deuteronomy 24:1–2. A written decree of divorce from the court always permitted remarriage, and was only necessary if remarriage was a desired future option for the parties involved (Deut. 24:2).

Another misused text on this subject is Matthew 5:31–32, where the term "putting away" (Greek *apoluo*) is often interpreted as "divorce" (*apostasion*). This makes it appear that Yeshua is condemning divorce and remarriage. This is an unfortunate misunderstanding of both the language and the culture of the Second Temple period, one which causes many to live in turmoil. A paraphrase of this text in its cultural context could better read: "The Law says that she commits adultery if she remarries without a written bill of divorcement, but I say unto you that whosoever puts her away (without divorce papers, which is against God's law) causes her to commit adultery (if she remarries under such conditions), and the man who marries her is also guilty."

Yeshua's clarification of this offense was given to help abused women, since the man in ancient society was generally not considered guilty for putting away his wife and marrying another. In such cases, the wife was often put out of the house without an official divorce. Yeshua is saying if a man does this, he is just as liable for adultery as the woman is. Yeshua further stated that a man marrying a woman who was not properly divorced (but rather put away) was committing adultery because he was marrying another man's wife. These issues were aimed at specific cases well known to Yeshua's listeners, and it is difficult for modern analogies to be drawn from them. The details of ancient divorce and remarriage with the related laws and customs are addressed in my lectures on the Book of Matthew.[6]

Many clergy, as well as laypersons, have thought that Yeshua made divorce synonymous with adultery. Nothing could be further from the truth. It is quite clear from Jewish law that God permitted divorce and remarriage in cases involving incest, beatings, and other abuses that caused one party to break other laws of God in order to remain married. In Luke 16:18, Yeshua dealt with a common first-century problem, one which his Jewish listeners clearly understood. In Yeshua's day, there was a common Jewish law, derived from biblical precepts, which stated that a man could not divorce his wife in order to marry his paramour.[7] Yeshua was addressing a specific problem prevalent in his day. He was not addressing the general categories of divorce and remarriage, which were not in question.

Both in Luke 16 and in the parallel text of Mark 10:11, the subjunctive mood (a verb whose action depends on a condition being met) suggests a specific purpose behind Yeshua's statement, and it is not to be treated as a general statement concerning divorce and remarriage. The idea is that the marriage bond should be maintained without an extramarital affair. The laws of God do allow for remarriage, but this text addresses the situation of a married man or woman who sees a more preferable partner. If a divorce is sought in order to be with that new partner, it is considered the same as adultery.

It should be emphasized that divorce was granted as a safeguard against abuse, and not for the sake of convenience. Although there is much controversy over this issue, a careful study of biblical divorce and ancient customs will show that God allowed divorce as a protection. It was never God's highest design. Although it is not God's "best," neither is it a transgression of any of God's laws, as is often thought today. There are only 613 laws and this is one of the positive ones, carried out only in cases of mistreatment in order to save life, or to spare the abused party further indignity.

Teaching Review, Chapter Five

1. It was a requirement for a believer in ancient times to give to the
_____.

2. The first priority was for the believer to give to the poor among his
_____.

3. This form of giving is called _____, taken from the root of the word for doing a _____ deed and it was to be done in a friendly manner with encouraging words.

4.   Ancient Jewish literature treated the person who hid his eye from the poor seeking help as a _____.

5.   The Apostle Paul exhorted that the greatest of the gifts are faith, hope and charity, and along with this concept he taught that _____ takes precedence.

6.   As believers, we are not to _____ fellow believers with our words or actions.

7.   There is special attention given to believers' responsibility not to offend, hurt, neglect, criticize or mock _____, _____, the blind and deaf.

8.   List the five different widows mentioned in the New Testament:
   a.   Widows who have _____ or _____, or has _____.
   b.   Widows who are _____.
   c.   Widows who give themselves to _____.
   d.   Widows more than _____ years old.
   e.   _____ widows.

9.   It is a negative commandment for any believer to tell anyone _____ things which another person said about them (Lev. 19:16).

10.   It is commanded that believers should not refrain from _____ one's fellow man from _____ (Lev. 19:16).

11.   As believers, we are not even to leave the _____ of a fellow believer crouched in a painful situation (Deut. 22:4).

12.   A believer is forbidden to ignore a _____ without returning it to the owner (Deut. 22:1–3).

13.   It is forbidden for a believer to destroy the _____ land or trees even during wartime (Deut. 20:19).

14.   The believer is required to make _____ provisions around his dwelling to remove the potential of an _____ (Deut. 22:8).

15.   List the nine different types of lusts mentioned in the biblical text:
   a.   Lust to destroy (Exod. 15).
   b.   Lust for _____ _____(Deut. 14).
   c.   Lust for what is not _____ (Ps. 106).

d. _____ lust (Matt. 5).   xt:
e. Lust for the _____ of the _____ (Mark 4).
f. Lust of the _____ (John 8).
g. _____ lust (Rom. 1).
h. Lust to _____ (Rom. 7).
i. Lust to have your _____ _____ (Titus 3).

16. It is forbidden for believers to commit _____
_____ or kidnap any living person (Exod. 20).

17. It is forbidden to hate a brother or do anything to cause him to
_____(Lev. 19).

18. It is forbidden to curse or appoint a corrupt _____ (Deut. 1).

19. In giving to or supporting the poor, ancient believers were not permitted to
charge _____ on a _____ to a fellow believer (Exod. 22; Deut.
23).

20. A believer could not _____ _____ of a loan from another believer when he did not have the funds to pay the debt (Exod. 22).

21. The employer was commanded to let the employee _____ of the produce in
which he was working.

22. The employer was required to give _____ to an employee on the
same day it was earned, if he was in need and asked for it (Deut. 23).

23. To nullify a vow an ancient Jew had to come before a *Bet Din*, or a
_____, of at least three judges who were well acquainted
with God's Law (Num. 30).

24. As part of ancient pledges, a _____ of some important object was
made to guarantee payment. A believer was not allowed to take any utensils used
to support a family or a poor _____ (Deut. 24).

25. It was forbidden for a believer to _____ in presenting a vowed or
voluntary _____ (Deut. 23).

26. The early church obviously had a _____ system within the congrega-

tion like the Jewish pattern of the synagogues. The Jewish rule was: "He who tries a cause before the Gentiles, this is an _____ man" (Sanh. 26:7). This is the idea we see Paul establishing at Corinth (1 Cor. 6:1).

27. God's laws were so detailed that they included provisions for _____ so much that it was forbidden to take _____ from a nest in the presence of a mother bird (Deut. 22).

28. A believer was forbidden to muzzle an ox while it was working in the _____ (Deut. 25). Paul used this well-known example to illustrate the caring for workers in the ministry (1 Cor. 9; 1 Tim. 5).

29. Believers were forbidden to leave a _____ animal in a ditch or in _____ (Luke 14; Exod. 23).

30. There are _____ different animals listed in Scripture, and God not only had Adam name each one, but declared that his covenant _____ them (Gen. 2; 9; Matt. 10; Luke 12). The biblical text records that the _____ individual regards the life of and cares for his animals, while the wicked do not (Prov. 12).

31. The believer was commanded to _____ and to sanctify the home with true love unless there was a biblical reason for avoiding it.

32. In ancient marriage contracts, the husband was obligated to provide his wife with what three major things?

   a. _____   b. _____   c. _____

33. On a much broader level, these three major concerns include various laws of the sages. These laws of the sages involve all the biblical principles, and are summarized in seven marital obligations:

   a. The husband pays for the _____.
   b. He must provide for _____.
   c. He must pay ransom if she is taken _____.
   d. He must _____ her.
   e. She is permitted to stay in his _____ all her days.
   f. She is sustained out of his property.
   g. Her _____ are cared for out of his funds.

34. There are a number of sexual abuses listed in the biblical text in order to safeguard a believer from falling back into pagan sexual practices associated with _____.

35. The sexual things that are forbidden include what is called a "forbidden _____ relation," when a believer has a relationship with one of his _____.

36. If a male believer has a sexual relationship with another male, he is to bring a _____ (Lev. 18:22).

37. If a man seduces a virgin who is not engaged to him, in ancient times he had to pay a _____ of _____ shekels of silver and, if her father would permit it, he was to _____ her (Exod. 22). This was equal to approximately _____ days of work at common labor.

38. Although _____ was permitted in antiquity, it was never God's intention. Kings and spiritual leaders were not to have more than one _____ at one time (Deut. 17; 1 Tim. 3).

39. Since _____ worship in ancient times included pornography in forms of statues, sexual symbols, and cult prostitutes (allowing people to pay tithes in heathen temples through _____), there are many decrees from the Lord warning against these pillars, groves (*asherim*), and obelisks.

40. In ancient times it was forbidden to _____ any male creature due to the fact that such action rendered it unfit to be used in the _____ as a sacrifice or servant (Lev. 22).

41. If there was an unbiblical abuse in the marriage, a divorce could only be obtained by the parties' going to a _____ _____.

42. The often misquoted text of Malachi 2:16, which appears to read, "For I [God] hate divorce," is actually misused. That text actually states that God hates the pagan custom of not biblically divorcing, but simply _____ _____ or turning out a wife without the fair treatment of a religious court. This passage of Scripture was referring to believers' following the pagan practice of putting away their Jewish wives to marry _____ _____.

43. Another often-misused text on divorce is Matthew 5:31, 32 where the term _____ (Greek *apoluo*) is often interpreted as divorce (*apostasion*), making it appear that Yeshua is condemning divorce and remarriage. Yeshua's clarification of this abuse was given to help _____ women, since the man in ancient society was generally not considered guilty for just putting away his wife and marrying another.

44. Because of a cultural difference, some modern theologians have thought Yeshua made divorce and _____ synonymous, but nothing could be further from the truth.

45. In Luke 16:18, Yeshua is dealing with a familiar first-century problem, where a man could not divorce his wife in order to marry his _____, and not the general divorce and remarriage situation (Sotah 5:1).

46. In both Luke 16 and Mark 10, the subjunctive _____ suggests a specific purpose behind Yeshua's statement that is not to be treated as a general statement concerning divorce and remarriage.

47. Biblical divorce was granted as a safeguard against _____, not for the sake of _____.

48. Although divorce was never God's best, and was only to protect the innocent, neither is it a _____ of any of God's laws.

CHAPTER 6

Conclusion

God's Kingdom is to be Separate

The Kingdom of God can be summarized in three elements: righteousness (doing God's Laws), peace, and joy in the Holy Spirit (Rom. 14:17). The New Testament lists ten categories of individuals who will be shut out of the Kingdom of God. This is Paul's way of saying the sins that pagan society endorses will not be tolerated in God's Kingdom (Eph. 5:5; 1 Cor. 6:9).

According to Athenaeus, the Ephesians were addicted to luxury, effeminacy, and sexual vice. Aspasia (470 B.C.E.), a beautiful woman of the Socratic sect, brought vast numbers of beautiful women into the country as prostitutes. Demosthenes (384 B.C.E.), the Athenian orator, records: "We have whores for our pleasure, harlots for daily use, and wives for procreation of legitimate children and faithful preservation of our property."

It was against this ungodly background that Paul was establishing that God's Kingdom was different. The list given by the apostle is not intended to delineate certain sins that will shut one out of the Kingdom, but rather is an indictment against all things contrary to God's law (1 John 3:4). Paul simply highlighted those sins that were not considered wrong by the pagans. As Kingdom people, we are to "walk and live in God's Spirit." This is the Jewish way of saying "do only things pleasing to God," which means only those things that do not violate any of his laws (Gal. 5:23–25). In order to fulfill this directive, one has to know the Law. To this end, this volume has been compiled for easy access to the 179 basic non-Jewish rules of God's Kingdom.

Walk in the Spirit

As Kingdom people, we are to walk and live in the spirit by not transgressing God's laws. Although there are laws, or rules, in every kingdom, God's laws are clearly given to make our lives more productive and joyous (Ps. 1; 150; Rom. 7:12,14). The biblical text indicates the only bondage related to God's law is when we break it and put ourselves outside the protective boundaries established by the Lord (1 Tim. 1:8; 2 Tim. 2:5). In such cases, the King has provided forgiveness to the repentant, and subsequent restoration of his Kingdom benefits.

Teaching Review, Chapter Six

1. The Kingdom of God can be summarized in three elements:

   a. _____   b.   _____

   c. _____

2. According to Athenaeus, the Ephesians were addicted to luxury, _____ and sexual vice. It was against this ungodly background that Paul was establishing that God's Kingdom was different. These sins were not the only ones that kept individuals from God's Kingdom, but simply highlighted those sins that were _____ considered _____ by the pagans in his society.

3. The terms "walking and living in the Spirit" are the Jewish way of saying live according to God's _____ and do those things that do not violate his _____ (Gal. 5).

4. God's laws are clearly given to make our lives _____ and _____ (Ps. 1; Rom. 7). The biblical text indicates the only bondage to God's Law is when we _____ it and put ourselves outside the protective boundaries established by the Lord (1 Tim. 1:8; 2 Tim. 2).

GLOSSARY OF TERMS

Aggadah: The non-legal contents of the Talmud and Midrash (commentary), including the ethinical and moral teachings. This information is usually given in the form of parables, stories, and legends that are used as teaching tools.

Amidah: The standing prayer known as the *sh'moneh esreh* or the "eighteen benedictions."

Apocalyptic: Ideas and teachings pertaining to the revelation (apocalypse) of the last days and the end of the world.

Apocrypha: The body of Jewish literature written between the second century B.C.E. and the second century C.E. that is not included in the canon of the Hebrew or Protestant Bible.

Boethusians: A religious-political party in the century preceding the destruction of the Second Temple and for some time afterward. Members were associated with the high priesthood and were closely identified with, although not identical to, the Sadducees and Herodians.

Chukim: A Hebrew word meaning "decrees."

Eduyot: A Hebrew word meaning "witnesses," used for such commandments as the *mezuzah* and the *tefillin*.

Essenes: A Jewish religious sect that flourished in Israel during the last two centuries B.C.E. and first century C.E. The derivation of the name is the Greek translation of the Aramaic or Syriac equivalent of the Hebrew word *chasidim*, meaning "pious."

God-fearers: A name used to describe the non-Jews in ancient times who believed in God, attended synagogue, prayed, feared God, and gave financially, but did not take the final step of circumcision (Acts 10:22).

Halakhah: A Hebrew word for religious law or legal rulings.

Hillel: A Pharisaic religious teacher and Sanhedrin head during the first century, who held a more liberal view of the Law than the Shammaites. Hillelites were students who followed his school.

Messianist: An early name for an individual following Yeshua (Jesus) as the Messiah.

Mezuzah: The Hebrew word for "doorpost," used for the small parchment on which the first two paragraphs of the *Sh'ma* prayer of Deuteronomy 6:4—9 and 11:13—21are inscribed. A mezuzah is affixed on the doorposts of Jewish homes in accordance with the concept of Deuteronomy 6:9.

Mikveh: A Hebrew word meaning "the gathering of waters," but used to refer to the ritual immersion of persons or utensils for purity.

Mishnah: A rabbinic textbook giving the essence of Oral Law, which, according to Jewish tradition, was handed down to Moses along with the written Law at Sinai. The Oral Law, or Mishnah, describes how to do what is commanded in the Law.

Mishpatim: A Hebrew word meaning "judgements," used to refer to moral or ethical laws.

Qumran: The site of the caves where the Dead Sea Scrolls were discovered, along the western bank of the Dead Sea. The home of a major group of Essenes from the second century B.C.E. until the war against Rome (66—73 C.E.)

Remez: An ancient form of Jewish exegesis in which the teacher used a veiled allusion back to another text. This method was known as "hinting" back to a certain Scripture or reference.

Shammai or Shammaites: A Pharasaic religious teacher and Sanhedrin head during the first century who held to a stricter view of the law than the Hillelites. Students who followed his school.

Sh'moneh Esreh: The ancient Jewish prayer known as the "Eighteen Benedictions," prayed each day by observant Jews.

Sicarri: A name of Latin origin, used by Josephus for Jewish patriots who maintained active resistance against the Roman government of Judea, and Jewish collaborators with it, during the Herodian period (6—73 C.E.). The name is derived from the Latin word *sica*, denoting a "small, curved dagger." In Roman usage, "Sicarri" referred to those armed with such weapons and was synonymous with "bandits."

Sukkot: A Hebrew word meaning "tabernacles." This is the name of one of the three pilgrimage festivals held each year in Jerusalem. Sukkot, or Tabernacles, begins on the fifteenth day of Tishri (usually in September) and lasts seven days.

Tallit: A four-cornered cloth used by Jewish men as a prayer shawl, as mentioned in Numbers 15:38.

Tefillin: A Hebrew word for the "phylacteries" worn on the head and arms of Jewish men over the age of thirteen, based on Exodus 13 and Deuteronomy 6.

Zealots: A group of extreme and uncompromising partisans in the cause of Israel's freedom from Rome. They refused to bow to any government or power other than God. They hated Rome and even fought against their Jewish brethren who sided with Rome during the decades of the Second Temple Period.

NOTES

Chapter 1—The Kingdom of God

1. *Babylonian Talmud (b.) Berakhot* 2a; 12b; 13a; 14b; *b. Yoma* 85b.
2. *Encyclopedia Judaica* (Jerusalem: Keter Publishing, 1978), 2:43–44.
3. *Seder Zera'im Berakhot* 12a.
4. *Mishnah (m.) Ta'anit* 3:8.
5. William Whiston, trans., *Josephus: Antiquities* (Philadelphia: Winston Company, 1969), 14.22–24.
6. Esd. 1:28–30.
7. *Exodus Rabbah*, vol. 3 of *Midrash Rabbah* XXIII: I, 279. Translated by Rabbi Dr. S.M. Lehrman (London: The Soncino Press, 1983).
8. *Berakhot* 5:5.
9. *Ta'anit* 23a; *b. Berakhot* 10a.
10. Roy Blizzard and Yavo, Inc., *Yavo Digest 4*, no. 3; (1989).
11. Solomon Schechter, *Aspects of Rabbinic Theology* (New York: Schocken Publishers, 1961), 87.
12. Robert Lindsey, *Jesus* (Jerusalem: Dugith Publishers, 1972). (Out of print clarification on David Flusser's book *Jesus*).
13. Roy Blizzard and David Bivin, *Understanding the Difficult Words of Jesus* (Dayton, Ohio: Center for Judaic-Christian Studies, 1984), 88.
14. Brad Young, *Jesus, the Jewish Theologian* (Peabody, Mass.: Hendrickson Publishers, Inc., 1977), 70.
15. *Ta'anit* 23a.
16. Hyman, ed., *Yalkut Shimeoni*, vol. 1, remez 766, p. 487. Also see Brad Young, "The Foundation of the Kingdom," *Yavo Digest 3*, no. 2. (1989), 9.
17. Solomon Schecter, *Aspects of Rabbinic Theology* (New York: Schoken Publishers, 1961), 83.
18. *Avot* 5:1.
19. *Berakhot* 7b.
20. Judah J. Slotki, trans., *Numbers Rabbah*, vol. 5 of *Midrash Rabbah* (London: Soncino Press, 1983), 30–32.
21. Roy Blizzard, "History of the Church, level I" (lecture presented at the University of Texas, Austin, Tex., 1986).
22. Rabbi Ishmael, Horovitz and Lauterbach, "On Exodus," *Yavo Digest 3*, no. 4 (1989).

Chapter 2—The Jewish Meaning of the Kingdom

1. Roy Blizzard and Yavo, Inc., *Yavo Digest 3*, no. 2 (1989).
2. *Berakhot* 2:2, 5.
3. *b. Shabbat* 153b.
4. Ephraim Urbach, *The Sages: Their Concepts and Beliefs* (Jerusalem: Magnes Press, 1975), 400.
5. *Jubilees* 12:19.
6. *b. Sukkah* 42a.

7. *m. Tamid* 4:3; 5:1.
8. *b. Berakhot* 10b–11a.
9. *m. Avot* 3:5, 6.
10. William Barclay, *The Mind of Jesus* (San Francisco: Harper Collins Publishing, 1976), 9.
11. Matt. 6:33; Brad H. young, *Paul the Jewish Theologian* (Peabody, Mass.: Hendrickson Publishers), 122.
12. 1. Macc. 3:18.
13. Ibid.
14. 1. Macc. 4:10.
15. 1. Macc. 4:24.
16. 1. Macc. 4:55.
17. 1. Macc. 12:15.
18. *Encyclopedia Judaica*, 7:682.
19. R.J. Zwi Werblowsky, ed. *The Encyclopedia of the Jewish Religion* (New York: Adama Books, 1986), 229.
20. *m. Avot* 1:3; 1 Macc. 3:50.
21. Sifre Deut. 323: 138b.
22. *Jerusalem Talmud Berakhot* 4b, chap. 2, hal. 3; also see Brand Young, *Jesus and His Jewish Parables* (New York: Paulist Press, 1989), 197.

Chapter 3—An Introduction to Understanding God's Laws (Kingdom Rules)

1. Ray Comfort, *Ten Cannons of God's Law* (Bellflower, Calif.: Institute in Basic Life Principles, 1992).
2. Ibid.
3. Ibid.
4. Ibid.
5. Ibid.

Chapter 4—Personal Obligations to God

1. H.A. Wolfson, trans. Philo, *Foundations of Religious Philosophy in Judaism, Christianity and Islam* (Cambridge, Mass., 1962), 164.
2. *b. Ta'anit* 2a.
3. *Avot* 1:5.
4. *Manual of Discipline*, Dead Sea Scrolls.
5. *Kiddushin* 40b.
6. *Ketubot* 111b; *Chafetz Chayim Mitzvoth*, p. 31.
7. *b. Pesachim* 109; *Tehillim* 104:15.
8. *b. Succah* 5:1.
9. *Pesachim* 109; *Chagigah* 6; *Kiddushin* 34; *Orach Chaim* 529.

Chapter 5—Proper Relationships Among Believers

1. John Lightfoot, *Comment on the New Testament from Talmud and Hebraica*. Vol. 4 (Peabody, Mass.: Hendrickson Publishers, 1979), 200.

2.   Adam Clarke, Clarke's Commentary Vol. 6: *The New Testament of Our Lord and Savior Jesus Christ* (Nashville, Tenn.: Abingdon Press, 1830), 217.; John Lightfoot, *A Commentary on the New Testament from the Talmud and Hebraica*, Vol. 4 (Peabody, Mass.: Hendrickson Publishers, 1979), 200–202.

3.   Barnes' notes on the New Testament (Grand Rapids, Mich.: Kregel Publishers, 1974), 712.

4.   *Ketubot* 47; *Orach Chaim* 240; Chaim Chafetz, *Concise Book of Mitzvoth* (New York, Feldheim Publishers, 1990).

5.   *Shabbat* 110b.

6.   *Matthew*. Course by Ron Moseley at the Arkansas Institute of Holy Land Studies, Sherwood, Ark.

7.   *Sotah* 5:1.

BIBLIOGRAPHY

Apocrypha. Cambridge: Oxford University Press, 1970.

Barclay, William. *The Mind of Jesus*. San Francisco: Harper Collins Publishing, 1976.

Blackman, Philip, ed. *Mishnah*. New York: Judaica Press, 1983.

Blizzard, Roy Jr., and David Bivin. *Understanding the Difficult Words of Jesus*. Dayton, Ohio: Center for Judaic-Christain Studies, 1984.

Blizzard, Roy Jr. lecture, "History of the Church," Austin: University of Texas, 1986.

Chafetz, Chaim. *Concise Book of Mitzvoth*. New York: Feldheim Publishers, 1990.

Charlesworth, James H., ed. *Old Testament Pseudepigrapha*. Vol. II. Garden City, NJ: Doubleday & Co., 1985.

Charlesworth, John H., and Loren L. Johns, eds., *Hillel and Jesus: Comparisons of Two Major Religious Leaders*. Minneapolis, Minn.: Fortress Press, 1997.

Clarke, Adam. *Clarke's Commentary*. Nashville, Tenn.: Abingdon Press, 1830.

Cohn-Sherbok, Dan. *The Blackwell Dictionary of Judaica*. Oxford: Blackwell Publishers, 1992.

Comfort, Ray. *Ten Cannons of God's Law*. Bellflower, Calif.: Institute in Basic Life Principles, 1992.

Encyclopedia Judaica. Jerusalem: Keter Publishing House, 1972.

Epstein, Rabbi Isidore, ed. *Soncino Talmud*. London: Soncino Press, 1948.

Flusser, David. *Jewish Sources in Early Christianity*. New York: Adama Press, 1987.

Hyman, A., ed. *Yalkut Shimeoni*.

Ishmael, Rabbi, Horovitz & Lauterbach. *The Mekhilta on Exodus*. New York: Jewish Theological Society of America, 1969.

Lightfoot, John A. *A Commentary on The New Testament from the Talmud and Hebraica*. Peabody, Mass: Hendrickson Publishers, 1979.

Lindsey, Robert. *Jesus*. Jerusalem, Israel: Dugith Publishers, 1972.

Moseley, Ron. *The Spirit of the Law: Should Christians Reject God's Law?* North Little Rock, Ark: Mozark Research Foundation, 1993.

————. *Yeshua: A Guide to the Real Jesus and the Original Church*. Baltimore, Md.: Lederer/Messianic Jewish Publishers, 1998.

Neusner, Jacob, ed. *Jerusalem Talmud*. Chicago: University of Chicago Press, 1990.

Schechter, Solomon. *Aspects of Rabbinic Theology*. New York: Schocken Publishers, 1961.

Slotki, Judah J. *Daniel, Ezra and Nehemiah: Hebrew Text & English Translation with an Introduction and Commentary*. London: Soncino Press, 1951.

————, trans. *Numbers Rabbah*, Vol. 5 of *Midrash Rabbah*. London: Soncino Press, 1983.

Urbach, Ephraim. *The Sages: Their Concepts and Beliefs*. Jerusalem: Magnes Press, 1975.

Werblowsky, R. J. Zwi, ed. *The Encyclopedia of the Jewish Religion*. New York: Adama Books, 1986.

Whiston, William, trans. *Josephus*. Philadelphia: Winston Company, 1969.

Wolfson, H.A., trans. Philo, *Foundations of Religious Philosophy in Judaism, Christianity and Islam*. Cambridge, Mass. 1962.

Young, Brad H. "The Foundation of the Kingdom." *Yavo Digest 3*, no. 2 (1989), 9.

———. *Jesus and His Jewish Parables*. New York: Paulist Press, 1989.

_____. *Jesus the Jewish Theologian*. Peabody, Mass.: Hendrickson Publishers, Inc. 1995.

———. *Paul the Jewish Theologian: A Pharisee Among Christians, Jews and Gentiles*. Peabody, Mass.: Hendrickson Publishers, Inc. 1997.